A ma chere Maman

HOW TO BE CHIC AND ELEGANT

TIPS FROM A FRENCH WOMAN

Marie-Anne Lecoeur

Table Of Contents

Introduction

Chic. What is it? It is not about trends, being fashionable and spending vast amounts of money on one's wardrobe. It is about knowing what to wear for each occasion, how to accessorise the outfits, the do's and don'ts of dressing well.

Chic is about simple lines, great cuts and classic clothes that we can wear for years. It is about understatement and simplicity.

Elegance. What is it? Elegance is about how we wear our clothes. It is about how we talk, how we walk and how we act in public. It is a whole attitude.

Chic and elegance go hand in hand in my book. We could be well-dressed but if we slouch, eat with our mouth open or swear a lot, sorry, but we will not be elegant. Elegance is the opposite of vulgarity. It is an attitude that keeps a bit of ourselves undiscovered. Who wants to know all the details of the last hangover? Keeping a bit of mystery is elegant. Too much familiarity is not.

What we wear can reflect our lack of taste and this will be emphasised if our personality clashes with our clothes. It is important to harmonise our look with our personality. For instance, if we wear clothes that are on-trend but better suited for a woman thirty years our junior, we will jar with our clothes and the total look will not work. We all know good and bad impressions are made in the first few seconds. So, it is important to give some thought to our appearance if we wish to make that all important, first impression, a good one.

It is amazing how wearing the right outfit can make us feel fantastic. It is a well known fact that when we feel good, we look happier and more attractive, bien sûr. This, in turn, will have a positive impact on our self-esteem. In our professional life, 'looking the part' will help us boost our confidence. Improving our self confidence will help us to achieve more.

Chic and elegance are not the prerogative of the rich. There is no point in spending vast amounts of money trying to emulate pop stars' outfits and achieving only one thing: a total lack of taste. At the other end of the spectrum many women of modest means look absolutely stunning in elegantly cut clothes, bought in the sales.

Enough of the platitudes and down to business. How do French women look chic and elegant?

They do not adorn themselves like a Christmas tree.

They do not wear overworked garments and clothes that scream 'tasteless'.

They do not wear too many colours at once.

They do not overdo the girly look either. You know the one, too much hair, too much makeup, too many frills, too much of everything.

They do go for classic styles, always.

They do choose classic colours, like black, navy, dark red, camel and white.

They do have a knack of looking well-dressed simply and effortlessly.

The following tips are not rocket science. They are borne out of my own experience growing up in France or picked up along the way while living in Jersey, in the Channel Islands.

Believe me, they are all tried and tested. I hope that they will help you avoid many style faux-pas and ease you into chic and elegance simply and effortlessly.

General Tips

♥ Tip 1: Mirrors
Please, please, please invest in mirrors, especially a full-length one. It is an ABSOLUTE ESSENTIAL. This is the only way you can judge at a glance whether your look is well coordinated from the top of your head to the tip of your shoes. Small mirrors will only show part of you: what you see may be great, what you do not may be a disaster. Do not leave your final check to the last minute in case you need to change your jacket, coat or shoes.

♥ Tip 2: Leaving the house
It is important that you give yourself a final check before leaving the house. Have a full length mirror in the bedroom and, if you can afford it, another by the front door. If your intuition says something is wrong, go back and get changed. Sorry if this sounds too drastic, but why step out looking less than great? Always listen to your intuition, it is never wrong. When it speaks to you, listen. I often change elements of my outfit, sometimes even the whole ensemble because it was not quite right. Nurturing a critical eye will ensure you do not commit a crime against good taste.

♥ Tip 3: Size

How can you hope to look great if your outfit is not comfortable, your trousers are too tight or your bra is squeezing your breasts so tightly that they are popping up to say bonjour? Your clothes have to fit your body shape and your size. Fidgeting with your clothes and not feeling at ease is not elegant. Elegance dictates that you know enough to wear the correct size.

♥ Tip 4: Weather

How can you hope to look chic in only a little top and skirt, with bare legs, in freezing temperatures? I do not know anyone who would find blue legs and chattering teeth a good look. Put your coat on.

♥ Tip 5: Do not let an outfit wear you

You should not disappear behind your outfit. You will never see a garish, multicoloured, over-the-top outfit on any French woman. We prefer simple, timeless styles. Less is definitely more, and that is our motto. I subscribe to the KISS principle: 'Keep It Simple Sister'. Wearing an over-the-top outfit can show a lack of confidence by hoping that the personality of the outfit itself will speak for you.

By wearing an outfit more suited to your personality, your confidence will increase and shine through.

♥ Tip 6: Confidence
If you wear the right outfit that shows your shape at its best, then you are bound to feel confident. Have no fear of being noticed. People will look at you because you are chic or elegant, and hopefully both. Hollywood stars look good on the red carpet because they pay stylists to choose the dress that will enhance their shape. Bad bits! We all have them. Learn to play them down and make the most of what you have. There is no perfect body, but you can make yourself look sensational.

♥ Tip 7: Simple lines
Please keep your look simple. Always. Leave frills and frou-frous for lampshades and bedsteads. Do not adorn yourself. Adornments will add inches to your size and make you look overdone. Stick to simple clean lines. Let the tailoring do the talking and let everyone's eyes do the looking. Every day is an occasion: dress for it.

♥ Tip 8: Role Models
To help you visualise chic and elegance, why not
build up a portfolio of photographs of style
icons? Coco Chanel who created the simple and
chic look at a time of frou-frous and frills,
Audrey Hepburn and her timeless look,
Katherine Hepburn, Grace Kelly, Jackie Onassis
to name but a few. I know that in the above list
only Coco was French, but you get the picture.
These women are all icons of chic and elegance,
long after their deaths. Study their photographs
and try to emulate their look. The idea is not to
become their double but to understand why they
became the epitome of style. Even though they
are from another era, their style is timeless.

♥ Tip 9: Savvy buying
Ask yourself these questions of EACH AND
EVERY purchase:
What is the quality?
Is it value for money?
How often will I wear it?
Does it purr classy or scream trashy?
Will it enhance my body and go with my other
outfits?

Remember, the lower the cost per wear, the better the value for money. For example, a dress costing one hundred pounds, worn ten times will cost you ten pounds per wear. However, a dress costing fifty pounds, worn only once will cost you fifty pounds per wear. I guess the hundred pounds dress was the better buy, non?

♥ Tip 10: Be ruthless
Be ruthless and take your time before making your decision. Buy in haste, regret at leisure. Do not let an assistant on commission push you into a purchase. A good sales assistant is worth her weight in gold: she will be honest and steer you towards clothing that suits you and away from mistakes. Develop a good rapport and you both benefit. No matter what the price, always be sure that you will wear the item and that it will be worth it. If it does not look good when you try it on, then put it back. If it does not appeal to you that much when you first see it on you, you are not likely to wear it often are you? Walk away.

♥ Tip 11: Heavy patterns
Stripes should be worn sparingly. Zebras are for the Serengeti. If you do wear a stripy piece, then the rest of the outfit should be understated.

A mixture of flowers on both top and skirt is a non-non. If in doubt, always keep to one motif or none. It is always best to err on the side of caution to avoid making unsightly mistakes. Causing hilarity is not how you want your outfit to be remembered. You do not want to stand out from the crowd for the wrong reasons. Less is more.

♥ Tip 12: Poise and grace
Elegant women are discreet: they know how to walk, sit and talk. They do not eat with their mouth open and do not yawn or cough without a hand in front of their mouth. They most definitely do not sit with their legs open. They do not swear, talk loudly or scream. They are poise personified. They attract admiration, not attention. Vulgarity is not in their vocabulary.

♥ Tip 13: Eating

We French women have a reputation for being able to maintain our weight even though we seem to eat everything and French dishes favour rich sauces, n'est-ce pas? However, our portions are on the small side. So we eat everything, but in moderate amounts. We do not pile up our plate with food and then go back for seconds. We eat at the table, not in front of the television, which adds elegance to our table manners. Eating is an important part of our day and so, sitting at the table makes for good social interactions with our family and friends. This special time is not just about eating but also spending time with our family and less about scoffing.

In France, we have our main meal at lunchtime, which gives us the rest of the day to eliminate those extra calories. Evening meals are usually light, such as soups or salads.

Although we adore food and our country is well-renowned for its culinary arts, we do not obsess with eating large amounts throughout the day.

♥ Tip 14: Too tight

Clothes that are too tight do not make you look slimmer but will only serve to remind you and everyone else that you are too big for the size you are wearing. This is definitely not a good look so you should steer well away from it. If your blouse gapes open over your breasts, if your skirt shows the outline of your knickers, or if your trousers give you a muffin top, your clothes are too tight. Get changed.

♥ Tip 15: Too short

Is your skirt riding so high up your thighs that it looks like a wide belt instead? Ditch it! This is neither chic nor elegant. It will not make you look sexy either. The only look you will achieve without any problem is cheap and vulgar. Ultra short skirts are a definite non in the elegance stakes. Come on, you deserve better than that. A pencil skirt just above, at or below the knee is so much sexier. Pair it with high heels and, oh là là!

♥ Tip 16: Age

Dressing up like your 15-year old daughter is not a viable option in my book, ma Chère. Please do not even try. It will NOT make you look younger, I promise you. You will only look ridiculous and desperate. As you get older, there is even more of a necessity to opt for classic cuts and lines. The shock factor may be acceptable for teenagers but not for mature women.

♥ Tip 17: Maintenance

Always cast a critical eye over your clothes. Get them mended, or if you can, do it yourself. Have that hem taken up, those buttons sewn back on, that seam repaired, you get the picture. Your clothes will last longer and, instead of hanging idle in the wardrobe, you will be able to wear them more frequently. For a unique look, try swapping buttons from old outfits to your new coat or cardigan. This will add a little je ne sais quoi to the outfit.

♥ Tip 18: Advice

Ask your hairdresser to show you how to tie your hair up in different styles. Ask shop assistants how to accessorise an outfit, or what colours to wear with that dress. Any assistant worth their salt would love to help you. Do not be shy to ask people for advice, as they usually love to help, moi aussi.

♥ Tip 19: Colours

Experimenting with colours is great fun but avoid wearing too many at the same time. Limit the number of colours on your outfit to a maximum of three. This also includes the colours of the accessories. For instance, outerwear: grey coat, red shoes, black bag and hat. Underneath: red blouse or top, grey skirt, black belt; or grey dress and red belt. Stick to one basic colour as the main part of your outfit: black, navy, cream (or beige), grey or red. Then accessorise this with one or two other colours, as in the above example. You will then be able to mix and match your clothes more easily and without having the need to buy new items all the time. You will always have something to wear.

You can wear black, white and grey with any other colour because they are not considered actual colours themselves.

The monochrome look is timeless.
Dark colours are slimming, so save these for the parts you wish to disguise. If your shape allows it, wear bright-coloured tops which will brighten your face.

♥ Tip 20: Colour tone
To make sure that you wear the colour or its tone that suits you, put the garment close to your face. Then look at yourself in a mirror: if you look drained and tired, then this tone is not for you. However, if your face looks healthy and glowing, you have found the right one. You can wear any colour, as long as it is the right tone for you.

♥ Tip 21: Cars
When getting into a car, wearing a dress or skirt, your derrière should go in first. Once you have sat down, keeping both knees together, pivot both legs into the car. Reverse the process when exiting. Et voilà! No more embarrassing moments revealing more than you want to.

♥ Tip 22: Trends

You do not have to follow trends blindly and buy every season's hot items. Select pieces which will match items already in your wardrobe, hot or not. Concentrate on developing your own eclectic style. Chic items from different eras can be matched together. The key here is to find a look that suits you and to make it your own. By following the tips in this book, you will be able to put any number of outfits together that will suit you and last more than one season. Some of my clothes are over ten years old and I get compliments every time I wear them. Mind you, they have probably become vintage by now, which proves the point I am making. Being chic and elegant is not about the current season and trend. It is about knowing how to create an outfit that works, about classic lines and simplicity.

♥ Tip 23: Walking

You must learn how to walk properly in both flats and heels. Please do not drag your feet if you wear flatties, it is definitely not elegant. Shuffling is not attractive.

When wearing heels, you should use your hips to give your walk a little wiggle to make you look more feminine. You have hips, use them to your seductive advantage. Why not spend a little time viewing 'how to videos' on YouTube? It will be time well spent.

♥ Tip 24: Tall and confident
Walk like a dancer, brace your abdominals and pull your shoulders back. Slouching will not show you to your best advantage. Be proud of yourself.

♥ Tip 25: Organisation
Organise the clothes in your wardrobe. After each season, sort your clothes out and give or throw away any that you will not wear again. Alternatively, you can raise money for your next purchases by selling them at a car boot sale or on Ebay. If you have room, move the clothes that are out of season in to the loft or another wardrobe.

Sort the clothes that are now in season. Wash, iron and mend them as necessary. I like to hang all my clothes in my wardrobe by colour, from light to dark. I do this with my dresses, skirts, blouses and jackets. You might choose to sort them by type (blouses, skirts, trousers, dresses) instead. Once you have organised your wardrobe the way you want, it will be much easier and less time-consuming to see what goes with what and to build any outfit at a glance.

♥ Tip 26: Planning

I like to lay out an ensemble first, usually on the bed. I can then check to see if it all works together. I put out the main item, whether it is a skirt, trousers or dress. Then I add the top, followed by cardigan, belt and other accessories. In this way, I can remove or add any item I wish and try different looks until I am happy. Remember not to wear an ensemble that you are less than enthusiastic about.

♥ Tip 27: The night before
Prepare your outfit the night before so that you have time to make sure that your accessories match, that nothing clashes and even your handbag is ready to go. How many times have we got ready too quickly and found, after leaving, that we have transferred only half the items from the bag we used the previous day? So irritating. Prepare the entire outfit, that means from the underwear to the accessories, the night before and you will be ready in a jiffy the next morning.

♥ Tip 28: Perfume
The best way to apply perfume is to 'mist and walk'. Spray in the air and walk through the cloud. One spritz is really all that you should use, as more could be overpowering. People gagging as you walk past is a sure sign that you have applied too much. For eau de toilette, you can stretch to two spritz, but only if it is delicate and without any alcohol. However, as a rule of thumb, you cannot go wrong with just one puff. For the same reason, do not over-apply your spray deodorant. Better still, use one of those sticks that do not leave a strong odour.

♥ Tip 29: Impulse buying

Do not buy any piece of clothing on an impulse, as nine times out of ten you will regret it. Even before whipping out your credit card, you should have already decided which outfit in your wardrobe this new piece will be matched to. This goes hand in hand with Tip 9 above. It is not rocket science. You should apply this rule to every purchase. In these hard times of economic uncertainty you owe it to yourself and to your bank account, to buy wisely.

♥ Tip 30: Sales

One last word: beware of the lure of the sales. Cheap is not always better. Just because an article is reduced does not mean that you should buy it. You are not making a saving, you are making a purchase. You need to remain a savvy buyer and the item still has to pay its way. Buy better quality bargains from higher-end shops instead.

Tips for Body Shapes

Apple

Your generous bust is accompanied by an equally generous tummy, which may give you grief when choosing the right clothes.

First: shapewear. These shaping undergarments will be extremely useful for you. They will give you a sleeker silhouette and smooth out those extra bumps under your clothes. Do not get dressed without them.

The trick for your shape is to balance the body and elongate it, with the help of V-necks, discreet vertical stripes and open jackets.

This can be done by wearing above the knee skirts with slimming tunics, V-neck tops with mid-rise boot cut jeans and A-line solid colour dresses. Layering also gives a great effect for your shape by wearing a light coloured top under a long sleeved jacket or button down top.

Big-Busted

Oh là là! You have it so you will always look ultra feminine, no matter what. But, as always, there are do's and don'ts.

The absolute first thing you MUST do is get your bust measured and invest in the best bras you can afford. They will change your look in seconds and your bust will look so much more inviting. It will also be kinder to your back.

Do wear feminine tops but avoid anything frilly, bright or patterned, as these will make your bust seem larger than it is.

Steer clear of anything too tight like corsets or unsupportive, like strapless little numbers. Of course, you can show some cleavage. Discretion is key here: you do not want to scare the horses. Choose structured tops or dresses, V-neck style. Dark colours will work best for your top as they are slimming. Use bright colours for your skirts and trousers. What about a silk, navy blouse with a red skirt?

Opt for simple and classic jewellery, and avoid large necklaces.

Hourglass

Hurray! You have a beautifully balanced shape, à la Marilyn. You can wear garments that will enhance your bust, waist and hips.

Tops and jackets that are fitted at the waist should be a staple in your wardrobe. Belts should also be worn at every opportunity to show off your womanly figure.

Steer well clear of frills and busy patterns, however. Make your shape speak for itself. Pencil skirts will look delicious with heels, of course. You do not need to wear anything too girly. Play with good cuts and colours instead. Let your figure do the talking.

Navys, reds and creams would look stunning on you. Black should be used sparingly as it would be a shame to hide your figure. I think, for you, trousers can be left in the shops. Dresses and skirts are a must.

One last note, do not overdo the makeup. You do not want to outdo Jessica Rabbit.

Pear-Shaped

The best thing to do for your shape is to balance out your top and bottom half so they are more in harmony.

Dark colours work best for the lower half as they are slimming.

Bootcut trousers and well-cut A-line skirts will invert the triangle of your shape. The skirt should not be too long, you do not want to look frumpy or dowdy, nor too tight, you do not want to emphasise your derrière.

Wear heels to elongate your figure.

Pear shapes usually have a slim waist so emphasising it is a good idea, but make sure that your top or blouse does not stop at hip level, as this is your widest area. Make the most of your lovely bust with scoop necks and bright patterns. You can be bold here with bright colours and eye-catching jewellery, to emphasise your upper half.

Petite

Good things come in small packages. The trick, to make the most of your shape, is to shop from specialised petite ranges, like www.boden.co.uk , www.precis.co.uk , www.asos.com/Women/Asos-Petite and www.minuet-petite.co.uk .
Petite clothing is cut in proportion to the petite frame. Garments are shorter than standard sizes, sleeves are shorter and lapels are slimmer. You no longer need to take your clothes to the seamstress to have them altered to fit you. They will have already been designed with you in mind.
You should avoid bulky fabrics, long skirts and large patterns. Any of these will swamp you and make you disappear. Accessories should also be pared down, no bulky necklaces or huge bags, for instance. Everything in proportion.

Slim

Slim women can get away with plunging necklines, backless tops, dresses and corsets to show off their athletic figure. However, you must still make sure not to show too much flesh. If shoulders, back or cleavage are on show, legs should be hidden in a long or knee length skirt or well-cut trousers.

A narrow waist can be shown off in fitted and belted knee-length skirts or dresses.

Trousers are best straight-legged or bootcut as the wide-legged variety could drown your slim frame. Steer away from large patterns for the same reason.

Tall

Tall women will find shopping in specialised stores less frustrating than standard shops as trouser and sleeve length will be right for them. Websites like www.longtallsally.com and www.tallgirls.co.uk will provide clothes tailored for your height and size: longer trouser length, tops with longer sleeves and waist lines sitting lower than on standard clothing.

How frustrating is it when you can find your 'size' but the garments still do not fit you? I always have trouble finding trousers that are long enough for me and I am not that tall at 5'8". Admittedly, shops have made an effort and have been offering trousers and jeans in different lengths for a while. But, it is still difficult for me to find what I call long 'smart' trousers. I would have to wear them bare foot for them to fit! I also find that, if you are tall, the length between your hips and crotch is longer than on shorter women and designers seem to forget that. I can recall a number of times when I found the right length trousers, only for these to ride so high up my crotch that it made me feel like I was sliding down a clothes line.

Try to avoid wearing the same colour on top and bottom. Break up your length instead with different colours and belts. Large patterns look good on you.

You can go for girly tops but stay away from crop tops and three quarter length sleeves.

Do not be shy to show off your long limbs. Short skirts look really good on you because, Honey, you have the legs. If you are older, skirts just above or at the knee are still extremely flattering on you. If you wish to shorten your legs visually, wear strappy heels, in a different colour to your dress or skirt.

Go for long slim trousers, with visible pockets. One last tip: do not slouch. Be proud of your height and walk tall!

Voluptuous

Having curves in the right places gives you an enviable figure. Two things are important for you: getting measured for your bras and wearing the right shapewear. They will lift you up and tuck you in as well as hiding any lumps and bumps. This will also make your clothes fit better. You will feel and look amazing.

Do go for simple, structured cuts, vertical stripes and open three quarter length jackets. V-neck tops and floaty blouses will look very good on you. Choose structured dresses or skirts worn with the right shapewear. If you go for floaty skirts, then pair these with high-heeled shoes or boots, not flat shoes as they will make you look stocky.

Anything with a belt would probably not be a good idea for your size. Different colours on top and bottom will make you appear larger and are a non-non. A one-colour outfit will make you look slimmer. Opt for a dark monochrome wardrobe with accents of bright colours in your jewellery and handbags instead. Certainly no froufrou, at any cost.

To finish off your outfits, longer length necklaces will look smashing with long but not overlong, earrings.

Do not wear anything short, stretchy or shapeless. Discard anything baggy, boxy and bulky. Stick to simple lines, without extra this and extra that. Less is more.

Please avoid T shirts (too tight), bright colours (too in your face) and dowdy skirts (too old). They will only emphasise your size and make you look boxy. It goes without saying that shorts, mini skirts and leggings are not for you. A list of things to give away to your friends or charity shops should include dainty jewellery, round necklaces, chokers and hoop earrings.

I know this list looks very restrictive but it is there to help you look your best. If you stick to classic cuts, darker colours, heels and good shapewear, you cannot go far wrong. The online shops you might like are www.simplybe.co.uk and www.curvety.com, whereas www.elegantplus.com contains a directory of plus-size shops. A word of caution, though, even though they cater for your size does not mean that you should buy with your eyes closed. Follow these tips, in order to make the most of your assets.

Tips for Clothes

Dresses

♥ Tip 1: LBD
The little black dress is not solely for evening wear. It can take you anywhere, from the office to the restaurant, by clever use of accessories for day or evening. Just above or just below the knee, in a simple shape that accentuates your waist or cleavage, discreetly of course, this wardrobe staple will never let you down. Just make sure that the size is right for you and not too tight.

♥ Tip 2: Coloured dresses
When choosing a dress in a bright colour, keep the cut classic and simple. In this way, the cut and colour are not competing for attention. Use sober accessories, so as not to gild the lily. Wear a simple belt in a colour that will either contrast or match the dress. It will add a certain je ne sais quoi to the ensemble. Finish off with a great necklace and heels, et voilà!

♥ Tip 3: Short-sleeved dresses

Short-sleeved, shift dresses are versatile and easy to wear. They are classically cut and can be worn in the office with or without a blouse underneath. Wear a cardigan in a complementary or contrasting colour over it, when the air-conditioning is blasting cool air. For instance, team up a grey dress with a belt and cardigan in colours of your choice. You are lucky here as grey goes with most colours. Shoes can either be grey or the same colour as the belt or cardigan.

♥ Tip 4: Wrap dresses

Wrap dresses are perfect to enhance a great décolletage but make sure the cleavage is not too deep. For a modest look in the office, a camisole can be worn underneath. Heels must be worn with this type of dress to carry it off. Flat shoes would make you look frumpy. You can now walk tall and show off your lovely curves.

♥ Tip 5: Barely there dresses

Choose dresses that show off only one part of your anatomy at a time. Show either your cleavage, your back or your legs, but absolutely not all at once. That would be a serious faux-pas. I am yet to see a woman in a low-cut, sleeveless, backless, short dress look chic and elegant. You do not want to send out the wrong message here. Parts of the body that are hinted at are so much more alluring. Showing less is more.

♥ Tip 6: Vintage dresses

Vintage dresses are great finds. You can breathe new life into them by adding a new belt, changing the buttons, or having them altered a little. The width of the skirt can be reduced or the sleeves shortened. Do not let little problems stop you from making that purchase. With a bit of tweaking, you can create a unique and stylish look.

Do not forget, if you know how to sew, there are many vintage patterns that can be bought online. Indulge your inner Mother Earth by recycling old garments, which would otherwise have been thrown away or forgotten in your auntie's loft. This option will not only give you an original look but will have the added bonus of saving you money. Not a bad thing.

Skirts

♥ Tip 1: Pencil skirts
Pencil skirts are my absolute favourite as they
emphasise a woman's curves without revealing
too much. You should own at least one of these,
in a basic colour. They come in many styles, split
at the back, at the front, or fishtail; but they are
all super-feminine. You can bring colour to the
outfit by wearing a blouse or top; or simply
match the main colour for a monochrome look.
Give your hips an extra wiggle with heels.
Parfait.

♥ Tip 2: Wiggle skirts
Go Sixties crazy with a wiggle skirt. This tighter,
below the knee variation of the pencil skirt lives
up to its name by adding the oomph to your
wiggle. Heels and simple accessories will finish
off this classic look. Stunning.

♥ Tip 3: A-line skirts
A-line skirts should be a wardrobe staple for
pear-shaped women. The wide lower part
diverts the eye away from the hips and bottom.
Keep the length just below the knee or the effect
will be lost.

♥ Tip 4: Long skirts

Women can be so elegant in long skirts and dresses, as long as these are fitted to the body. If they are wide and ample, they will become dowdy. Please see the tip below.

♥ Tip 5: Full skirts

Full skirts, short or to the knee, are great for balancing out a large bust but will drown petite women. Remember Cousin It from the Addams Family?

Long, full maxi skirts are, in my opinion, dowdy because they swamp the figure down to the feet. Add a flowery motif along with flat shoes and you too could star in The Little House on the Prairie.

♥ Tip 6: Puffball skirts

Puffball skirts are not what I would call elegant as the cut is neither classic nor simple. They do not complement any woman's shape. If you wish to go for the pumpkin look, (always very popular on Hallowe'en) and have a big derrière and wide hips, it is up to you, but I would not recommend it.

♥ Tip 7: Short skirts

Every woman should avoid skirts that are too short. Here I am talking about micro minis, that finish just below your buttocks. More like a belt than a skirt.

On the other hand, mini skirts, which finish mid-thigh, can look fantastic on young women with long slim legs. However, if your legs are not up to par, mini skirts should not be in your wardrobe.

As you get older, lengthen the skirt a bit, even if you have fabulous pins. The shortest you could get away with is a couple of inches above the knee, even with opaque tights. Less is always more in my book, but short skirts are the exception that proves the rule.

Suits

♥ Tip 1: Suits

Every woman should have at least one suit. I prefer a skirt or a dress suit to trouser suits as these can look too manly. Trousers have their place in our wardrobe of course, but generally, we can leave them to the men.

Be selective with the jacket, as you want it to suit your body type. A jacket that is fitted will show off a figure beautifully. A long, loose one will hide it. Be confident about your womanly shape and do not keep it hidden under loose clothing. Short jackets should be avoided by apple shapes and larger women.

♥ Tip 2: Colours

The most wearable colours are the ubiquitous black, navy and grey. Be careful with the navy, though, as it has a tendency to look like a uniform if the cut is not stylish. Worn with a blouse, shirt or simple top, in a contrasting colour, the suit will be a very good investment and should last a number of years. Heels are of course de rigueur, the height is up to you.

Sweaters & Cardigans

♥ Tip 1: Sweaters

Sweaters are essential to own in classic or bright colours. Black, navy and red will take you anywhere. Roll necks are super elegant but will emphasise a large bust.

I do not see the purpose of cropped sweaters. A sweater is to keep you warm, so why wear one that covers only part of your torso? It makes no sense to me. So, drop the crop.

♥ Tip 2: Cardigans

Cardigans are versatile and, in my view, indispensable. You can have them in any colour you wish. However, classic colours are essential for versatility and matching the rest of your wardrobe. You can wear them over a sexy little camisole, with a few buttons open and just the lace of the camisole showing. You can wear them over a dress or over a blouse with a pussy-bow tie. This looks really feminine.

Cropped cardigans, as opposed to cropped sweaters, work well over dresses as, here, your torso is covered by the dress.

By the way, I mean slim little cardigans here, not the big thick wooly variety. You do not want to go out looking like the best in show. Keep these for cosy winter nights by the fire. They will keep you nice and snug.

Trousers

♥ Tip 1: Cut and length
Trousers should be well-cut and long enough,
which can be a problem for long legged women.
Not too long or your hem will drag on the floor
and become frayed, or worse get caught in your
heels going down stairs. Not too short or you
will look like you sprouted overnight. The
perfect length depends on the height of your
shoes. If you are lucky enough to find the perfect
cut for your figure, think of buying different
lengths for different heels.

♥ Tip 2: Black tailored trousers
Black tailored trousers are one of the most
versatile elements of your wardrobe. They will
take you anywhere and can be worn with any
top, blouse, shirt, sweater or cardigan. A must-
have for anybody's wardrobe. You know, I have
not yet found the perfect pair for me. The hunt is
still on!

♥ Tip 3: Jeans

Jeans are essential but must be chosen with the same discernment as any other item. You have to cut your way through a forest of many different styles.

They can look very stylish worn with heels or ballerina pumps, a crisp white shirt and brown leather belt. It is a cliché, I know, but this look works.

Make sure they flatter your derrière. For a flat bottom, go for jeans with flapped pockets. If you are rounded, pockets with motifs will bring even more attention.

As always, they must be the right size. If you have to lie on the floor and use a coat hanger through the zip to pull it up then, Houston, you have a problem.

♥ Tip 4: Pirates

Short, wide trousers never ever look good on anyone. Unfortunately, they are worn by hordes of women every year. Why look like an extra from a Pirate film? I have yet to see even one woman looking good in them. They are not shorts because they are too long. They are not trousers because they are too short. They are neither one thing nor the other. Why not wear shorts or trousers instead?

♥ Tip 5: Shorts
I do not own a pair of shorts. Get the hint?

♥ Tip 6: Harem pants
These are another style of trouser to avoid. They have no redeeming feature; the low hanging crotch does not flatter the figure in any way, shape or form. Leave these for the souks of Marrakech.

♥ Tip 7: Leggings
Oh mon Dieu! In a word, dreadful. If they are to be worn, they should be teamed with a long top, tunic or dress over them. Absolutely NO short tops, this does not leave anything to the imagination. Your bottom, in all its glory, would be on display. All in all, not a good look. One last thing, please no white leggings either, aaargh. This is a crime against style.

Coats

♥ Tip 1: Quality
We all need to own one good coat, the best that we can afford. It will be worth its weight in gold as it will be worn every day for a few winters. So, quality is especially important. You want a coat with a high percentage of wool, as it will keep you warm. So will cashmere. Cotton lets the cold through. Do not skimp with a cheap, thin coat as you will regret it on bitterly cold days. Make sure you buy one in a basic colour that will go with most of your winter wardrobe. Matching, or contrasting gloves will be an elegant accessory.

♥ Tip 2: Pear shapes
If you are pear-shaped, choose a coat with detailing on the collar or shoulders to bring the eye up and away from your problem area. Also ensure that they are fitted at the waist and double-breasted. Check the rear view to ensure the back pleat or slit does not gape open. Avoid coats that are full at the bottom.

♥ Tip 3: Petite

For petite women, even if buying from specialised shops, be careful to avoid long and bulky coats that would swamp you. Aim for knee length and you cannot go far wrong.

♥ Tip 4: Large busts

Single breasted coats look good on you. Make sure there is no detailing in the bust area, such as pockets and wide lapels.

Colours

♥ Tip 1: Red

If you have the figure for it, dare to wear red as it can look stunning. A dress or skirt in a passionate, luscious red really stands out and can look ever so chic. An added bonus is that it attracts men.

However, if your shape does not allow this bright colour on your clothing, what about a red scarf, handbag or lipstick instead?

♥ Tip 2: Bright colours

Bright colours go well together but remember no more than three on the same outfit. Include a basic colour as part of these three, such as white, cream, navy, grey, black, so as not to make the outfit too busy.

Tips for Lingerie

Now you are talking… Everyone loves beautiful underwear. My favourites are of course matching sets. They always look good together. Underwear does not have to be only sexy, as comfort is extremely important for our delicate areas. However, comfort does not mean settling for bland and boring.

♥ Tip 1: Bras
We are so spoiled for choice out there but the first thing to do is to get yourself professionally measured for your bras. An ill-fitting bra does not make the most of the bust and makes the breasts look saggy. If the bra is too small and tight, it will give you more lumps and bumps than the Michelin man. A well-fitted bra, on the other hand, will improve your posture and make you look confident and proud. Walk tall.

♥ Tip 2: Uplift
Why resort to painful breast augmentation surgery when you can use padded, push-up, balcony and plunge bras? These cleverly designed accessories will make you feel and look uplifted in a jiffy. If you have a beautiful athletic figure, why go under the knife?

♥ Tip 3: Sports bras

Wear a sports bra when practising sports, obviously. Breasts bouncing up and down when you are jogging are uncomfortable, and moreover, can damage the elasticity of the breast tissue. Ouch!

♥ Tip 4: Generous busts

If you are endowed with a generous bust, you are the lucky ones who do not need the help of push-up bras. As before, the vital thing for you to do is to get your bust measured and buy the best bras that you can afford for your size. These should have wider straps to ensure that the extra weight is distributed over a wider surface and do not dig into your shoulders. They should support you well and give you a neat outline. This is extremely important for your back and your bust.

♥ Tip 5: Try before you buy
Whether balconnette, strapless, multiway or low-front, you can now find a bra to wear under any type of dress or top. The trick is to take your new dress or top with you when shopping for the bra to wear with it. Try them both on in the changing room to make sure you buy the perfect bra for it.

♥ Tip 6: G-strings
G-strings should not show over the top of your trousers or jeans, as you bend down. Cheese wire anyone? Why not try low-rise shorts with jeans instead? They come in every colour and material and their shape makes them extremely comfortable to wear. Perfect for jeans.

♥ Tip 7: Styles of lingerie
Try to avoid garish colours. Opt instead for style but do not let that stop you from being adventurous.
Remember that there is a difference between lingerie that is designed to be worn and lingerie intended to be taken off. Choose accordingly!
If you have the means to splurge: splurge. The detailing in good quality underwear is exquisite and worth the expense.

♥ Tip 8: Erotic lingerie
Avoid any lingerie labelled 'erotic'. You want to look sexy, not vulgar. Elegance and crotchless do not belong in the same sentence.

♥ Tip 9: See-through fabric
Believe it or not, white underwear does show through white fabric. If you wear unlined white trousers or skirt, your underwear should be flesh-coloured, so as not to show under your clothes. What is elegant about a black G-string showing under your white trousers? Nothing.

♥ Tip 10: VPL
You have spent a fortune on clothes which sculpt you, give you a wonderful contour and an enviable silhouette. Spoiling this effect by wearing unflattering underwear would be such a shame. To avoid extra lumps, bumps and lines, seamless knickers are a girl's best friend.
Let us rebel against visible pantie lines.

♥ Tip 11: Two for one
A sensible thing to do, when buying a bra and knicker set is to buy two pairs of knickers (Brazilian and thong for instance). This way, it will give you more flexibility to wear the set with different outfits.

♥ Tip 12: Labels
There is nothing like a label showing through your lacy bra or sticking out of the back of your knickers to spoil the effect of your beautiful underwear. You already know your size and the brand. Just cut the pesky thing off.

♥ Tip 13: Delicates
Wash both bra and knickers from the same set at the same time, or you will end up with a bra of a more vibrant colour than your knickers.
Washing lingerie by hand in cold water or on a delicate machine cycle is a necessity. Place them first in a laundry bag for even more protection.

♥ Tip 14: Slips

Shops seem to be selling many dresses at the moment, which is great. What is not so great is that many of them are unlined and I think that is a shame. Lining provides an extra layer to protect you from the 'Diana effect' in the sun. It will also prevent your dress from clinging to your legs due to static. The only thing to do is to wear a slip underneath. The overall look will be neater and less embarrassing.

♥ Tip 15: Shapewear

To disguise lumps and bumps, wear shapewear or support garments that every underwear brand or department store now stocks. Shapewear is currently big news and more user-friendly than it used to be. Some of them are even sexy too. You can now find body-shapers, control bodies, hourglass corselettes, thigh slimmers and spanx.

For easy shopping, try the following online shops: www.cassshapewear.co.uk (where you can browse by body shape) ,
www.figleaves.com/,
www.ukSimplyyours.co.uk,
www.shapewearonline.co.uk, and
www.themagicknickershop.co.uk, to name but a few.

Shapewear can be worn by any shape to disguise minor or major bumps and other unsightly embonpoint, to flatten your tummy or give you an hourglass figure. Magnifique! Forget the instruments of torture which were worn by our long-suffering great-grandmothers. New shapewear is now made of soft and comfortable fabric, like spandex, silicone and stretch lace, so can be worn every day. They are so well designed that they are invisible under your clothes and will give you a most enviable figure. Why avoid wearing an exquisite dress when you can look sensational with these little helpers?

♥ Tip 16: Silk
In closing, spoil yourselves, or better still, get spoiled by your loved one, with pure silk underwear. There is nothing like luxurious silk on your skin to make you feel beautiful.

Tips for Shoes

Shoes! My favourite subject. We all adore shoes. There is so much to say about shoes that I thought they deserved their very own chapter. Is it because our feet do not put on weight and always stay the same size? Whether we gorged ourselves at Christmas or lost weight by eating healthily again?

The right pair of shoes will always makes a woman's legs look good, no matter what. The important word here is 'right'.

♥ Tip 1: Comfort

Who says that fashion has to be painful? Believe it or not, shoes have to be comfortable. This is quite difficult to achieve, I know, as the market is inundated with badly made shoes. They have to be comfortable because they support the whole weight of your body. If you are on your feet all day, then this is essential. The way to ensure that you buy comfortable shoes is by trying them on around the shop for longer than a quick look in the mirror and a short trip up the aisle. I know we feel like muppets, nobody walks around in new shoes in shoe shops anymore, right? Take them for a test drive around the shop for a few minutes. It can be a bit embarrassing but it will save you money in the long run. As you walk, concentrate on how they feel. Obviously, you will have chosen them first on how they look on your feet and eliminated the ones that look ridiculous.

Ask yourself these questions:

- Do they pinch any part of the foot?
- Does one shoe feel comfortable while the other pinches?
- Does the strap feel too tight or too loose around the ankle?
- What about the height and the width of the heel?

If you are going to walk any distance, forget about impossibly high heels. They may look great in photo shoots, but in reality, they will damage your feet and you will find it difficult to walk elegantly in them. You get the picture.

♥ Tip 2: Styles
It is better to wear your old shoes than invest your hard-earned cash on a new pair that does not fit properly and is painful to walk in. You will not wear them and it will be a waste of money. They should make you feel elegant and feminine.

Clumpy shoes are a big no-no as they make you look, well, clumpy.

Wedges and platforms usually seem to suit younger women.

Women of all ages look stylish in court shoes with a sexy heel. A sexy heel does not have to be six inches high, just not clumpy. Make sure when wearing heels, that you know how to walk properly in them. Use your hips when you walk, that way you will not walk like a duck. Use your beautiful hips and give it a wiggle like Marilyn, woohoo!

♥ Tip 3: Abomination

I hope that, if you are reading this book on chic and elegance, you are not wearing those ugly slouchy boots. You know the ones I mean! These do absolutely nothing for the woman wearing them. They only make her look like a fashion victim. Please keep away from these, they are an abomination.

♥ Tip 4: Sandals

Flat sandals have their place during hot summers or on holiday. Again, the rule to apply here is comfort, especially if you do a lot of walking. However, why give up on style? You will need something that gives your foot support for walking but makes your foot look slender and lovely. Please do not forget that, with more of your foot on show, you have to paint those toenails and remember your heel care.

♥ Tip 5: Gladiators

Gladiator sandals are not stylish in my view. They may look good on Russell, but will they do the same for you? They have too many straps that bind around the ankle and make the foot look clumpy and shorten the leg. Something that shows more of the foot will be sexier.

♥ Tip 6: Winter
Do not mix sandals with winter clothes. I know this sounds obvious but believe me, I see this every year. Surely, if it is cold enough to wear a coat, it is cold enough to cover your feet. As always, dress for the weather.

♥ Tip 7: Ankle straps
Ankle straps cut across the ankle and make your legs look shorter. And yes, this even applies to women with long legs. We all like strappy shoes but lower placed straps are a better choice to elongate the whole leg.

♥ Tip 8: Ballet pumps
Ballet pumps are certainly comfortable. However, they will look out of place on apple, pear shaped and large women. The proportions will be wrong and will make you look stumpy. To elongate your silhouette, wear pointed shoes with a heel.

♥ Tip 9: Ballet pumps 2
On the subject of ballet pumps, try to get the ones with a little heel. This will prevent the skin on your heels from cracking.

♥ Tip 10: Boots

Long, tight leather boots look good on any woman with a skirt or dress in the winter. Go for high-heeled boots rather than flat ones, as otherwise you may look like you are off to the stables. Wear them with a long coat or short jacket. Patterned tights peeking out at your knees will add allure. One last word of caution, thigh length boots send out a different message. Flat-heeled and you look like a pirate, high-heeled give you the working girl look.

♥ Tip 11: Sizes

Women with big or small feet may have trouble finding shoes in their size. The High Street generally only caters for the average. We all have to fit into their range of sizes: 4 to 8 for shoes and 8 to 16 for clothes. Thanks to the internet, we can now find everything we want at the touch of a few buttons, from the comfort of our own homes.

Shoes in large sizes can be found at:
www.bigshoeboutique.co.uk ,
www.after8shoes.co.uk ,
www.totallylargeshoes.co.uk ,
www.parrisshoes.com , www.longtallsally.com ,
www.amberandjade.com .

For small shoes online, go to
www.petitfeet.co.uk ,
www.piccolosmallshoes.com , www.pretty-
small-shoes.com , www.smallmeasures.co.uk .

♥ Tip 12: Longer legs
To give the illusion of longer legs, the trick is to
match the colour of your shoes with the colour
of your legs. Wear nude shoes with nude tights
or bare legs, or black shoes with black tights.
You get the idea.

♥ Tip 13: Little toes
Shoe designers sometimes forget that women
have five toes. Some of their pointed shoes are so
narrow that you would need to be a creature
with four toes to squeeze your feet into them.
Incredibly, some women do have their little toes
surgically removed in order to wear them. It is
time for designers to realise this fact and for us
to vote with our feet! Out with the impossible to
wear and in with the comfortable yet chic.

♥ Tip 14: Labels

Please remove the ugly stickers from the soles of your shoes before you wear them. These little suckers look unsightly and are difficult to remove. There are label-removing products on the market you can use.Your look could be absolutely flawless from the front but not from the back. Labels will spoil the effect.

♥ Tip 15: Smelly feet

To remove unwanted smells from your shoes, sprinkle one teaspoon of bicarbonate of soda inside each shoe and leave overnight. Remove before wearing. Problem solved.

♥ Tip 16: Shoe care

To nourish your leather shoes, apply a good polish of the appropriate colour and leave overnight. Buff up the next morning with a soft cloth. You can also make them shine, believe it or not, with the inside of a banana skin. It works a treat.

Some shoes come with shoe trees and stretchers. Use them.

If you are caught out in the rain, dry your shoes carefully and stuff them with newspaper to absorb the moisture. Leave to dry naturally, not on top of a radiator.

If you have listened to my advice so far, you will know by now that, by choosing a classic look, you can wear your shoes and boots for years to come as their style will be timeless. Kerching!

♥ Tip 17: Repairs
Have those heels repaired when you can hear the clank of metal on pavement. Your shoes will last longer and you will achieve a more polished look. This also goes for scuffed heels. If these cannot be repaired, I am afraid that you will have to ditch them. It is better to wear cheap but unscuffed shoes than expensive but scruffy ones. Roughen up the smooth sole of your new shoes to avoid slipping or have anti-slip soles fitted. It is difficult to remain dignified on your derrière!

♥ Tip 18: Barefoot
Last, but not least: Do not walk barefoot in the streets. You could injure yourself on uneven pavements or cut yourself on shards of glass. The soles of your feet will become caked in black sticky muck, which will take you ages to scrape off. Walking barefoot in your house or garden is one thing, walking willingly among all sorts of waste is another. Please take care of yourself, and that includes your lovely feet.

Tips for Accessories

We all know that accessories can make or break an outfit. Your outfit can look plain without any or over the top with too many. Get it right with a little scarf expertly tied around your neck or a hat framing your beautiful face. A little goes a long way.

Be your accessories' harshest judge. The look you are after is chic and elegant. This means style, simplicity and symphony. It does not mean fancy, fuss and fanfare.

Simplicity is key here. It does not have to be boring. It screams great cut, quality material and style. In France, you will often hear women mention buying a 'simple' T-shirt or a 'simple' dress. It shows that they have good taste by avoiding the OTT. It will also be more economical as these simple garments will match and go with the rest of your clothes. Just change your accessories for a different look, et voilà!

Jewellery

♥ Tip 1: Coco's tip

With jewellery, as with everything else, the less is more approach is important. It is said that Coco Chanel recommended looking at yourself in a mirror just before leaving the house and removing one item of jewellery or accessory. If it is good enough for Coco, it is good enough for us, non?

♥ Tip 2: Bare minimum

If you are going to wear only one item of jewellery, earrings on their own will do nicely. It shows that you care but do not want to look overdone.

♥ Tip 3: Pearl earrings

To be chic without looking like you are trying too hard: wear pearl earrings. If they are the only accessory you wear, then you cannot go wrong with these. They denote a subtle touch of class, effortlessly.

♥ Tip 4: Coloured studs
If you wish to add a touch of colour around your face, studs that pick up the colour of your dress or blouse or your other accessories, such as belt and scarf, work well.

♥ Tip 5: Hoop earrings
Steer away from huge hoop earrings if your aim is to be elegant. Tarot readers we are not. Understatement always works best for all occasions, except for the Carnival in Rio.

♥ Tip 6: Bold jewellery
Necklaces finish off an outfit but they have to add to the elegance, not jar with the style. There is a vast array of jewellery out there and we are spoiled for choice, so choose wisely.
Always question your potential purchase.
What dress, sweater or blouse will this necklace enhance?
Is this piece of jewellery too dainty or too bulky?
How many bangles should I wear?
The less, the better, is the obvious answer.
Bold jewellery can be stunning as a statement. However, please tone down the rest of your outfit to show it off. One piece that stands out is the limit or you will look overdone.

♥ Tip 7: Quality not quantity

Aim to own timeless pieces of jewellery, such as pearls, diamonds and a good quality watch. Always buy these from reputable jewellers. You may think that this is extravagant or beyond your means but if you refrain from buying low quality items, the money you save over time will enable to you to invest in them. They are stylish, as opposed to trendy, and thus will last for a lifetime. Do not be a magpie attracted to every shiny thing. Quality, not quantity.

♥ Tip 8: Colouring

Just as there are colours in clothing that will suit your skin colour, choose the colour of your jewellery in the same way. For example, yellow gold does not suit me at all. I wear silver, white gold or platinum instead. If you have blue eyes, diamond or sapphire earrings will be for you. If you have green eyes, emerald earrings can have a stunning effect. Diamonds and pearls suit everybody, Dieu merci.

♥ Tip 9: Proportions

If you are petite, try to steer away from large pieces of jewellery to maintain a sense of proportion. If you are used to wearing large pieces of jewellery, try to reduce the size. Choose thinner necklaces.

Larger women should not go for too thin a necklace. Also remember that chokers emphasise the width of the neck so should be avoided. Go for longer pieces that elongate the neck and bring the eye down to the decolletage.

♥ Tip 10: Pearls

Wear your pearls! They are the quintessential accessory. They look good even if you are naked! Single, double or triple strand necklaces, earrings or bracelets: wear them and enjoy them. They add a subtle sexiness to any ensemble. Buy the best quality that you can afford as you will not regret it. The more you wear pearls, the better they look. Take good care of them and they will give you that love back tenfold.

♥ Tip 11: Discretion

I cannot emphasise enough the 'less is more' approach. This means no multitude of bangles up your arm, no diamanté tiara or chandelier earrings. Elegance goes hand in hand with discretion. One single bracelet will finish off your look better than a cacophony of bangles. If you wear those charm bracelets that are all the rage at the moment, remember to wear simple sleeves and no other fancy jewellery.

♥ Tip 12: Patterns

If you are wearing a top or blouse with detailing, like a pussy-bow tie, or printed tops, then only wear discreet earrings. Leave off the necklace as it will be lost among the detailing or pattern.

♥ Tip 13: Piercings

I know you can attach all sorts of accessories to your body but do you really have to go the whole hog by adorning all your body parts with jewellery? I mean, nose rings? Tongue studs? Eyebrow pins? None of these have ever, EVER shown any hint of elegance whatsoever. Please do not make holes in your body unnecessarily, you will no doubt regret it in later years. Have you ever seen a granny with a ring through her nose or trying to manoeuvre her tongue stud between her false teeth? No, neither have I. On the subject of tongue studs, not only can they make it difficult for you to be understood as it gives you a lisp, but they also damage tooth enamel. Discoloured teeth are not a good smile accessory.

Hosiery

I love wearing hold up stockings. Tights can be too constricting around the waist, and let us face it, even though they are extremely practical, they are not what I would call the sexiest of garments. Stockings are far too fiddly to put on when hurrying to get ready for work. Unfortunately, hold ups can have the unwelcome habit of not 'holding up'. This is sometimes due to having been washed too often, or because you have put cream on your legs. I once had the misfortune of having one hold up sliding its way down to my knee. I ended up having to walk home whilst holding the top of it through my skirt. How elegant is that? I now choose my hold ups with care. Examine the tops: the elasticated top and silicone band have to be wide. That is what keeps them in place. If they are too narrow, they will not have the 'hold up' factor and will invariably slide down, as you walk. Zut alors!

Hats

I am so glad to see that hats have finally made their comeback. Hats can look very chic and set off an outfit really well. Wide brims also protect the head and the face from the harsh rays of the sun. A wooly hat is absolutely necessary in winter.

Some people feel that they do not have a head for hats. I disagree. There is a hat out there for you. I assure you, there is a style for everyone. Just persevere and you will find the style that is made for you.

♥ Tip 1: Size
It is essential to try hats on for size. The hat, whatever its shape or style, has to fit your head snuggly. It should not be so loose that it falls off if you look down, or so wobbly that you end up wearing it sideways if you turn your head quickly.

♥ Tip 2: Jaunty or not?
You can wear hats straight on the head, tilted to one side at a jaunty angle, or low at the front. Your hair should be tidy underneath and show at the front or back. Use hat pins for those windy days.

♥ Tip 3: Berets
A beret can be worn to the right or to the left, but definitely not flat on the top of the head, or you will look like a drawing pin. Do not, under any circumstances, wear a beret with a navy and white stripy top. No, not even in France.

♥ Tip 4: Baseball caps
Leave baseball caps to sportsmen. They are not chic, they are not elegant, they are not stylish.

♥ Tip 5: Panache
A hat of any style should be worn with panache. Try not to feel self-conscious, even if you are not used to wearing one. Stand tall, take a deep breath and be proud of yourself. With the right hat on, you will look fabulous.

Scarves

♥ Tip 1: Square
A small, square scarf tied to the side of the neck can finish off an otherwise plain or dark outfit. Choose one with a motif if the outfit is plain, vice-versa if the outfit is patterned.
In windy weather, a large one can also be worn over the head as follows:
1.Make a triangle of the scarf
2.Place it over your head with the right angle pointing to the back
3.Frame your face with the other two sides
4.Cross over the two side points under your chin
5.Tie them neatly at the back over the point at the base of the neck
6.Wear with sunglasses for the Grace Kelly look.

♥ Tip 2: Shawls
What about a large silk or wool shawl? These always look great, and on any occasion. Wool shawls can even be worn over the shoulders or the head when the weather is especially bitter, while still remaining chic. Silk shawls are preferable for evening wear.

Belts

♥ Tip 1: Essential
Belts can change an outfit instantly and as such, you should keep a good selection in your wardrobe. Large, thin, colourful or neutral. Do not throw away a belt because it is last season. Belts come in and out of fashion very quickly, so keep them in your wardrobe. Once you have established your own style, you no longer have to be a slave to trends anyhow. Wear them when you want to.

♥ Tip 2: Body shapes
Petite women should go for slim belts, worn with heels, to elongate the figure.
Boyish figures should go for large and colourful belts to help give them a waist.
Marilyn types can wear belts either high up to showcase their bust or low down to show off their sexy hips. Be careful about the width of the belt: not too wide is best.

♥ Tip 3: Substitutes

Try substituting one of your own belts around your coat or trench coat for a different look. The belt will need to be large and in one of the basic colours, navy, black, red or cream.

Handbags

Handbags are very much like shoes. We go crazy over them. We covet them, love them and cherish them till debt do us part. We have black ones, cream ones and blue ones. We have square ones, round ones, and shapeless ones. We have small ones, long ones and huge ones. But, no matter how many we have, we can never have enough. We fall in love at first sight and we have to have them there and then. The last bag we buy will be our favourite...until we cast our beady eyes on the next one.

♥ Tip 1: Quality
Try to invest in one high quality, classic leather bag, that will transcend the seasons and designers' latest whims. Choose it in a classic colour that will go with most of your outfits. Check the seams, zips, handles, straps and the inside too. If you are paying big bucks for it, you have to make sure that the bag is well-finished and has no obvious flaws.

♥ Tip 2: Staples
Aim to own a bag in a basic colour from each of the main styles: the clutch, the Kelly, the shoulder bag, the tote and the hobo. These are the staples for different occasions.

♥ Tip 3: Proportions
Remember proportions? It also works with bags. Petite women should not carry huge bags and a tiny bag would make a large woman appear larger. Also, bear in mind that a large rounded bag will make your middle appear larger than it actually is.

♥ Tip 4: Draw bag
A little trick for when you switch handbags is to buy or make yourself a type of draw bag in a soft material. Put in all the regular things you normally 'lose' in your handbag, like purse, pen, lipstick, mirror, tissues and keys. It will be so much easier to transfer this draw bag into another handbag, in one fell swoop, with all the items in it. Do the same for your makeup that you carry with you and you will never leave anything behind again.

Tips for Sensational Skin

It is important to remember that being chic and elegant is not just about fashion, styles and clothes. It is just as much about your body. Your gorgeous clothes will not have the same impact if you do not look after yourself as much as your wardrobe. The tips in the following chapters are here to help you look as good as your clothes.

♥ Tip 1: Basics
The foundation of looking good is that the skin, especially the face, should always have clean pores, and be well-moisturised. Makeup should be removed at night and the face cleansed and toned. A good moisturiser should then be applied. Repeat in the morning. For the young ones out there, a light moisturiser is all you need, as anything too heavy may make your skin greasy and cause blemishes.

♥ Tip 2: Moisturisers
You do not have to spend a fortune on expensive moisturisers, as equivalents can be found for a fraction of the price. These are usually the ones which win prizes for the best moisturisers anyway.

Do not get fooled by clever marketing or attractive packaging when your budget is tight. Even olive oil is good for the skin, just put it on overnight and feel your soft skin the next morning.

♥ Tip 3: Cold water
A great natural way to tone your skin is to splash your face with cold water. Aaah, so fresh and invigorating. Do it ten times first thing in the morning to give your face a wake-up call.

♥ Tip 4: Scrubs

Why invest in expensive scrubs? You can either make your own by mixing cleansing cream and salt or use a face cloth instead. How simple is that? Ideally, face cloths should be rinsed without fabric conditioner so that they remain a tad rough. Wet the clean face cloth with hot water, not boiling please, and wash your face with it. The hot water will open your pores. Then, rinse the cloth with cold water, not freezing, and apply it to your face. The cold water will close your pores and tighten your skin. You can also give this treatment to the rest of your body, as it feels really invigorating. If you are not used to it, you will find the cold water a bit uncomfortable at first but if used every day, you will really come to enjoy it.

♥ Tip 5: Perky

While we are at it, finish off your shower by rinsing your breasts with cold water. This will perk them up no end.

♥ Tip 6: Dry brushing

Dry brushing your body with a natural bristle brush every morning before you shower is a marvellous thing to do. It not only removes dead skin cells, but also stimulates the lymph system and blood circulation. This rejuvenates your skin and prevents skin problems. Start at the bottom of your feet and work your way up towards the heart, avoiding your face, but finishing with your scalp. Incroyable!

♥ Tip 7: Hydrate

Drink water throughout the day, not just tea or coffee. This will not only eliminate toxins but will also hydrate the skin, giving you a healthy glow.

♥ Tip 8: Avoid blemishes

Try to avoid touching your face throughout the day as hands are covered in germs and dust. Touching your skin forces make up, grime and oil into the pores and causes blemishes. At the end of the day, place your face over a bowl of hot, not boiling, water for a quick and easy facial steam to unblock the pores. Splash with cool water to finish off.

♥ Tip 9: Acne

Natural remedies for acne are lemon juice, apple cider vinegar and cucumber juice. Give these products a go if you are plagued with spots. Soak a cotton wool ball with any one of them and apply to your skin. Aloe Vera is also good against acne and helps to reduce acne scars.

♥ Tip 10: Diet

It may have been said a hundred times before, but do try to improve your diet. Eat less greasy, fatty and sugary foods and more fruit and vegetables. Your skin will thank you for it.

♥ Tip 11: Bags

To get rid of bags under your eyes, lie down for 15 minutes with a cool slice of cucumber on each eyelid. Cucumbers have calming and toning properties. Have a few more slices at hand so that you can replace them as they warm up. It works.

♥ Tip 12: Avoid too much sun

It might be great for vitamin D but look after your skin by avoiding too much sun. You will be happier for it in your later years when your face does not show too many wrinkles. Let us be sensible here and take care of ourselves, no more frying please. Protect your skin by applying a cream with an SPF of 15 or above. Do this daily, even in winter.

♥ Tip 13: Fake tan

Please do not overdo it. A little goes a long way. My view is that they are better used, not to make you look tanned, but to stop you looking pasty. Orange is not a colour that looks good on anyone.

♥ Tip 14: Smoking
It used to be the height of chic. We now know
that smoking will age your skin prematurely.
Sucking on a cigarette will cause tiny wrinkles to
form around your mouth. It will also discolour
your teeth and skin and make your clothes
smell. Quel dommage!

♥ Tip 15: Alcohol
Alcohol causes broken capillaries and worsens
rosacea. Skin becomes dehydrated and coarse.
Avoid excess drinking if you want to keep your
skin beautiful, fresh and wrinkle free.

♥ Tip 16: Exercise
Regular exercise will stimulate your blood
circulation, which in turn will give you a healthy
glow. It also encourages, apparently, the
production of sebum, which is a natural body
moisturiser. Super, non? Exercise is also a good
pick-me-up. If you are happy, you will be more
likely to look after yourself and make the
necessary efforts to stay chic and elegant.
A brief workout before you dry brush your skin,
followed by a shower, will give you the best of
all skin colours: a healthy one. Give your skin
the best chance of looking good.

♥ Tip 17: Nourishment
Skin is more receptive to nourishment and regeneration at night. This is why we must not skip on night cream, especially when we are older. What a great feeling waking up in the morning, soft and moisturised. It is better than taut and flaky any time.

♥ Tip 18: Sleep
Let us have plenty of sleep: a minimum 6 hours a night is recommended. You skin will look healthier if you get plenty of rest. If you are going to be out late, have a catnap before getting ready.

♥ Tip 19: Ink

The plumage of a multicoloured parakeet peeking out from the back of an evening gown does not convey the right image. The look achieved is more akin to a butch sailor than the epitome of elegance. Many women later regret the tattoo of their ex's name on their shoulder, arm or buttocks: do not make the same mistake. Please think about how your tattoo will look when you are older. You may be thinking now that the design will make you stand out from the crowd; and you will be right. A rose bush climbing up your leg will definitely attract glances your way, but not for the right reasons. Ridicule and embarrassment are not what we are after here. So, if you have tattoos, keep them out of sight.

♥ Tip 20: Unwanted hair

Moustaches look best on men and hairy legs on tarantulas. Women, on the other hand, look best silky smooth.

We all have problems with hair not growing fast enough on our heads but no problem sprouting everywhere else. Removal is time-consuming and painful. However, you have to make sure that you keep your body hair shaved, waxed, depilated or plucked. Failing that, keep it safely hidden from view, et voilà.

Trimmed eyebrows give a finished look. Have this done by a professional now and again and you can just follow the main outline in between. Please do not overdo the arch: if you look constantly surprised, people will wonder why.

♥ Tip 21: Cellulite
Most women have problems with cellulite, we all know that. I wonder whether sitting on our derrière all day long at the office does not make it worse.

You can try to diminish cellulite by banishing fatty meals and sugary drinks from your diet. Therefore, dare I repeat myself, watch your alcohol intake. Sustained regular exercise is also recommended, such as walking, spinning or swimming. Three times a week is best, with sessions of at least 30 minutes each, as the body starts using its fat reserves after 20 minutes of exercise. Try to walk up the stairs instead of taking the lift, walk to work instead of driving or taking the bus.

♥ Tip 22: Botox & Collagen

Bee-stung lips and frozen features make you look like a caricature of yourself. Elegance is about getting old gracefully. There is nothing wrong with having a bit of 'work' done. However, it should only give you the 'back from holiday' look; you should still be recognisable to your own children.

Tips for Make-up

♥ Tip 1: Young skin

Make-up will look better and last longer on regularly cleansed and moisturised skin. Just like a painting will last longer, if painted over a good quality canvas. Be your own work of art, ma chère.

If you are young, do not smother your face with foundation. Young faces are wrinkle-free and beautiful all by themselves and do not require coverage, even in winter. It is such a shame to see young girls smothering their natural vitality; all because they look at too many photographs of overly made up celebrities in magazines. Remember, those celebrities are already older than you and need a little assistance to look as young by using make-up or airbrushing.

If the skin is cleansed every day and taken care of, there is absolutely no need for any coverage. The exception here is probably a concealer for blemishes that you may get from time to time. However, if the face is always hidden under layers of foundation, the skin cannot breathe and is bound to produce more unsightly spots.

♥ Tip 2: Older skin
As you get older, you might prefer to use foundation. However, I would not recommend wearing it every singly day, maybe for an evening out during winter, but that is all. A drop of foundation mixed in with moisturiser is enough. Alternatively, a tinted moisturiser can be used instead if your face looks a tad pasty.

♥ Tip 3: Coverage
If you use foundation or other types of coverage, please do not finish at the jawline as the neck will look too white in comparison. Avoid the Pierrot look at all costs. Make sure you fade this coverage into the neck as much as you can.

♥ Tip 4: Less is more
With make-up, the 'less is more' approach is even more important, especially true for daytime. Leave the full make-up for the West End stars. They need to be seen from the back seats of the theatre. You do not.

♥ Tip 5: Lips

Cracked lips make us look tired and ill. If there is only one thing that you apply on your face after moisturising, let it be lip salve. Vaseline is especially good. Moisturised lips look and feel good. Keep your lips hydrated and luscious for pouting, kissing and attracting envious glances. Oh là là!

♥ Tip 6: Longer lasting lipstick

To make your evening lipstick last longer:
1. Apply a light coat of foundation on your lips
2. Let it dry
3. Using a lipliner the same colour as your lipstick, trace the outline of your lips first and then apply to the rest of the lips
4. Apply a fine coat of loose powder on your lips
5. Apply your lipstick with a lip brush
6. Using a folded tissue, press your lips on it to remove the excess lipstick
7. Repeat from point 4 once

You will be amazed at how long your lipstick lasts. You can add some gloss in the middle of the lower lip as a finishing touch. Be kissable all night long.

♥ Tip 7: Lipstick on your teeth

Lipstick on your teeth? Sacrebleu! To avoid this situation, a simple trick: after applying your lipstick, put your index finger in your mouth, then remove it gently while puckering your lips around it. The lipstick that comes off on your finger could have otherwise ended up on your teeth.

♥ Tip 8: A touch of blusher

If needed, a touch of blusher or bronzer over your face in the morning or before you go out will make you look fresh and healthy. The operative words here are 'a touch', again less is more.

♥ Tip 9: Amazing eyes

Open up your eyes by using eyelash curlers on your eyelashes. Your eyes will stand out more. For a more dramatic effect, add a coat of mascara.

♥ Tip 10: Mascara tips

To ensure that mascara is applied right to the very tip of the lashes, apply it in a zigzag motion from the roots to the tips. This will ensure full coverage of every eyelash.

♥ Tip 11: Tired

Do not apply mascara on the bottom lashes if you look tired. Your tiredness will show up more as you will be emphasising the shadows under your eyes.

♥ Tip 12: Daytime make-up

For daytime, the discreet look is best. A light base or tinted moisturiser can be applied first to even up your skin, but only in winter. In summer, our skin is naturally tanned and looks better au naturel. Add a touch of blusher and eyeliner if you wish. Mascara and lipstick to finish off. The over-made up look does not work for daytime and you can only get away with it at night when the lights are dimmed. Less is more, remember?

♥ Tip 13: Evening make-up

For evening, you can experiment a bit more with eyeshadow and strong lipstick. However, there is a rule that we should all abide by: do not emphasise both your eyes and lips at the same time. If you choose to bring out your eyes with strong eyeshadow, eyeliner and mascara, then your lips should be fairly pale and discreet. On the other hand, if you wish to wear a bright or strong lipstick with lipliner, then the eyes should be toned down.

A mirror in your handbag, along with your lipstick for a few touch ups during the night, will be invaluable.

♥ Tip 14: Party make-up

For parties, the little black dress is usually de rigueur. The best make-up to go with that LBD will be an illuminating face powder, smoky eyes and red lipstick. And off you go.

♥ Tip 15: Excess of foundation

If you have overdone the foundation, to remove the excess, pass a moist sponge lightly over your face, then dab with a tissue.

♥ Tip 16: Eyeshadow base
To make your eyeshadow last longer, use a base or primer over your eyelids. This is great for parties that last until the early hours of the morning.

♥ Tip 17: Eyeliner
Lines made with eye pencils seem to fade very quickly. For a longer lasting effect, use a liquid or cream eyeliner instead. They are more difficult to apply if you are not used to them but the trick is not to produce the line in one go. Draw a series of dashes and then cover them with a final line.

♥ Tip 18: Staying power
Due to lack of moisture, dry skin is not able to hold makeup efficiently. To give your foundation or eyeshadow more staying power, apply some moisturiser or use a facial spray on your skin beforehand.

♥ Tip 19: Cleaning

It is vital to keep your brushes and sponges clean if you do not want bacteria breeding on your makeup. You could spread them on to your face, or worse, into your eyes. Clean your brushes and sponges regularly in four tablespoons of bicarbonate of soda mixed in a litre of water. Leave overnight. Rinse well.

♥ Tip 20: Concealer

Last, but not least, the concealer. This little matt corrector is a woman's best friend. Use it to hide those pesky red pigmentations, blemishes and other imperfections on your face. Always tap away the excess with your fingertips or a brush. Otherwise, you might just make a target of the blemish and attract more attention to it.

Tips for Hands and Nails

♥ Tip 1: Moisturising
Well-moisturised hands not only feel smoother and softer but they also look younger. They are not to be neglected as you reach your forties and beyond. Slather on hand and nail cream, morning, noon and night. You will not regret it. Try to wear cotton gloves over your freshly moisturised hands for a few hours or overnight. You will notice the difference.

♥ Tip 2: Almond oil
Massage your hands with sweet almond oil, which is rich in vitamins A, B1, B2, B6 and E. This will calm and soothe your skin, from the nails to the wrist; and the fragrance is divine. Magnifique!

♥ Tip 3: Exfoliation
Exfoliation is not just for your face. Use exfoliators and masks for hands once or twice a month for truly wonderful results.

♥ Tip 4: Chapped hands
During winter, your hands can become chapped if you do not wear gloves.
Try this simple remedy:

Make a soft cream with two teaspoons of honey
and a bit of warm water
Mix in two teaspoons of cider vinegar
Rub this cream into your hands
Leave for a few minutes
Rinse, dry and rub in your favourite hand
cream.

♥ Tip 5: Gardening
A special tip for the gardeners amongst us:
scratch the top of a bar of soap before gardening
if you really do not like to wear gloves. The soap
under the nails will protect them from becoming
black with dirt. Green fingers are one thing,
black fingers are another.

♥ Tip 6: Gloves
Wear gloves for gardening, washing up and
other domestic chores that involve water. You
can even apply moisturiser on your hands before
doing the washing up and the gloves will then
work in the moisturiser all the more.

♥ Tip 7: Cooking smells
It is hard to be elegant at your dinner party with hands reeking of certain cooking odours. The worst thing to do is wash them with hot water as the open pores will absorb the smells. To remove fish, onion and garlic smells from your hands after cooking, rub them with a stainless steel bar under cold water, like you would do with soap. This works by the sulphur compounds of fish, onion and garlic binding to the stainless steel, thus removing the smell from your hands. You can buy such an item from the excellent Lakeland company at www.lakeland.co.uk (available at time of print).

♥ Tip 8: Nail maintenance
If you have problem nails, do not hesitate to use the various nail products on the market to protect, repair and nourish them. They do the job they are supposed to do. A little care and attention are all that is needed.

♥ Tip 9: Nail file
Avoid cutting your nails, as it can weaken them. Use a nail file instead. File from the outside edge to the middle to avoid splitting them.

You will never regret keeping a nail file and a small tube of hand cream in your handbag for those little emergencies.

♥ Tip 10: Discoloured nails
Yellow or discoloured nails can be due to harsh cleaning products, low quality nail varnish or tobacco. To whiten your nails, soak your hands in tepid water mixed with lemon juice for five to ten minutes.

♥ Tip 11: Stronger nails
Here is a little known natural trick to strengthen your nails. Regularly massage the nails with the cut end of a clove of garlic. Remove the garlic smell by rubbing your hands on stainless steel under cold water, as mentioned earlier. For even more strength, regularly soak your nails in lemon juice, olive oil or salted warm water.

♥ Tip 12: Healthy looking nails
For healthy looking nails, soak them in tepid water mixed with sweet almond or other oils. Then dry your hands and carefully push your cuticles back with an orange stick.

♥ Tip 13: Daytime
For daytime, I recommend that you stick to a pale neutral or clear varnish for your hands. It is difficult to see peeling clear varnish but peeling red nail colour really screams 'cheap'. So keep your nails clean, nicely filed, and with a touch of clear varnish to make them shine. This is all you need to do.

♥ Tip 14: Longer lasting nail varnish
A little trick for your nail varnish to last longer, without peeling too soon, is to extend the top coat to the tip of the nail and then continue over the edge, ensuring that the cut edge is coated. It will then be more difficult for the varnish to peel off.

♥ Tip 15: Manicures
Manicures are an essential part of female grooming. You should aim to have a manicure at least four times a year, one at the start of each season. Avoid having more than one manicure per week, though, as it could weaken your nails.

You do not need to spend hundreds of pounds a month on manicures. You can just go to a salon before an evening out to have your nails shaped and coloured professionally. If money is tight, you can try to do it yourself, but it is always difficult to do your dominant hand. For this reason, clear varnish is better to self-apply than a full-on red as mistakes will not be as noticeable. For strong colours, better leave it to the professionals.

♥ Tip 16: French manicures
A French manicure looks really chic on every woman. It suits every occasion and every outfit. Odd-looking false nails and multicoloured nail art and glitter will clash with your style. Keep it simple, remember?

♥ Tip 17: Sandals

Bright reds, dark maroons, magentas, pale pinks and neutrals look best on toenails. If you wear sandals or open-toed shoes, do not leave your toenails plain. Always have a pedicure before wearing sandals for the first time in the spring or summer. If you do not have pedicures regularly, your feet will need it after a whole winter inside closed shoes. Invest in a heel scraper and use it daily. One minute every morning is all it takes. It is essential that your heels are always smooth in sandals, nobody wants to see your cracked heels poking through the back of your flip-flops. How unsightly!

Tips for Hair

♥ Tip 1: Glossy hair
To achieve a glossy look naturally, try the following: mix two teaspoonfuls of vinegar or the juice of one lemon into a litre of water for rinsing your hair after shampooing. Do not overdo the vinegar: you do not want to smell like your favourite takeaway.

♥ Tip 2: Smooth hair
If you wake up with bed hair in the morning, think about changing your cotton pillowcase to a silk one. Contrary to cotton, silk is so smooth that it does not ruffle hair.

♥ Tip 3: Swimming
Soak your hair with fresh water before entering the swimming pool or the sea. As the hair will be waterlogged, chlorinated or salted water will not be able to penetrate it.

♥ Tip 4: Curly hair
If you have curly hair, lucky you. To loosen up the curls a little, use a deep conditioner once a week, and detangle your wet hair with a wide-tooth comb. Use anti frizz products and refrain from washing your hair every day. Washing too often will dry it out even more and make it frizzy.

♥ Tip 5: Hair straighteners and curlers
Straightening or curling your hair is a quick and effective way to change your look before an evening out or just for the fun of it. Do not go overboard by doing it every day, as it can damage the hair.

♥ Tip 6: Updos
Updos are great but leave the complicated stuff for weddings, prom nights or Marge Simpson. Do not let your hairstyle dominate your overall look. Choose simple chignons or have your hair tied with a well-chosen comb.

♥ Tip 7: Ponytails

For the days when your hair is lanky and lifeless, you will achieve a more stylish look by tying your hair up in a simple ponytail rather than leaving it long. However, keep the ponytail low, to avoid the cheerleader look. Also, shun the root-damaging Croydon facelift by not pulling the hair too tight.

♥ Tip 8: Braiding

Holiday braiding may be a fabulous look while on the beach in Spain but is rather out of place in the office. What happens in Ibiza should stay in Ibiza.

♥ Tip 9: Hair accessories

There is a tremendous choice of hair accessories out there. The aim here is not to go OTT with huge purple flowers or diamanté angels perched atop your head. Go for classic and understated, not over-fussy.

♥ Tip 10: Hair extensions

The previous comment also goes for hair extensions. Please settle, as always, on achieving the natural look and use these to make your hair thicker but not obviously fake.

Believe it or not, extensions look far better in the same colour as your own hair. The real and the fake should match perfectly. Leave those long curly plastic locks on the shelves.

♥ Tip 11: Sun hats
We all love the sun but you would be amazed at how much it can bleach your hair. To retain the colour and prevent it from fading out or going brassy, wear a hat in the sun. It will also prevent sunstroke and sunburn.

♥ Tip 12: Shampoo
Do you know the trick that shampoo advertisers used for doubling the sale of shampoo overnight? They developed the phrase 'Rinse and repeat'. Well, unless you have been rolling in the mud, your hair will not need to be washed twice. One dose of shampoo and conditioner is generally all that your hair will need. As I said earlier, do not get fooled by clever advertising.

♥ Tip 13: Hair mask

Due to overuse of heating tongs, straighteners and curlers, our hair may need extra help to bring moisture back in. After massaging a deep conditioning mask well in to the hair and scalp, wrap your hair in a towel. Leave it for twenty minutes and rinse. After rinsing, your hair will be shiny and oh so soft.

♥ Tip 14: Wet hair

Whatever you do, do not go out with wet hair. It sends out the message that you are not organised, you have just got out of bed and are late for work. Please take the time to dry and style your hair.

♥ Tip 15: Colour

Hair should be clean. It should also be well-cut and dyed to hide any grey. Grey hair can look chic, as long as it is well styled. While talking about colour, please, please, please stay away from purples, pinks and other psychedelic hues; keep these for small accessories destined for the inside of your handbag.

Having your hair coloured by a professional is recommended. I know that going to the hairdresser's regularly is expensive, but you will have made savings anyway with the tips I am giving you, non? For a look that does not scream fake, ask them to aim for one to two shades lighter or darker than your natural shade. If money is tight, and you are doing the colouring yourself, use a colour not too different from your eyebrows. This will keep you within one to two shades of your natural colouring, which will suit your face.

NB: Please do test the colour first before doing the whole head, just in case.

♥ Tip 16: Roots

Avoid showing your roots by colouring your hair one to two shades lighter or darker, as mentioned earlier, so that the roots are not so obvious. Alternatively, touch up the roots yourself or visit your salon regularly.

♥ Tip 17: Bleaching

Over bleaching can give your hair a brassy appearance. In addition, do not become a bleached blonde if your eyebrows are dark. This will look odd. Your dark eyebrows will stand out like caterpillars.

♥ Tip 18: Haircut

A good haircut is worth a thousand hair accessories and the investment. It will flatter your face, make you look younger and, need I say it, sexier. If your hair is very fine or very thick, regular cuts will be wise, to keep it all in check. Choose your hairdresser wisely.

♥ Tip 19: Split ends

We are not friends with split ends. You may be proud of your long locks but the look will be spoiled by the split ends. Get your hair trimmed every couple of months or so for a healthy looking style. Your hair will look shinier and you will look better for it.

Split ends look like you do not care. The 'do not care' look is not what we are after here. You may really want to have long hair, and it can be traumatic to have it cut, but split ends will spoil the effect.

♥ Tip 20: Salons

Your hairdresser should be your friend. They should love your hair as much as you do and want to make you look gorgeous EVERY time. It is difficult to complain when you are not happy with your new cut or colour. But, if you dislike the way your hairdresser is styling your hair or the service is not good, go elsewhere.

I experienced a catalogue of mishaps with my old salon. I had colour dropped on my clothes and shampoo in my eyes. I ended up with hair colour that was darker at the ends than at the roots. The stylist would moan that my hair was too thin and had a total disinterest in me as a client. The last straw was when she pushed me into going blonde. Ah non alors!

I voted with my feet and have been a client of my current salon for over 15 years now. I have never regretted switching. James, my colour technician really knows his stuff and Jasmine is a talented stylist who always makes me feel like a million dollars. Your trip to the salon is so much more than just having your hair done. You deserve the best. Toujours.

Conclusion

If there are any tips that you should remember above all others, they should be:

Keep It Simple Sister
Less is more
Quality not quantity.

Yes, it can be an effort to be chic and elegant every minute of the day. It certainly takes an element of discipline. As women, there are many calls on our time such as home, children and work; but the effort is well worth it. We owe it to ourselves to look good whenever and wherever we are. Practiced regularly, you will find that some of the tips here are time saving, leaving you with more time for other things.
I hope that all of these tips will help you achieve a chic and elegant look every day. Bringing a touch of elegance to our streets is a welcome change. It is to be hoped that, with this change, we shall also see the return of respect towards women.
Be good to each other.

Also by The Author

How To Be Chic & Elegant: Plus Size

Are you plus sized or even just a bit overweight? Are you fed up of buying the wrong clothes for your shape?

Do you want to look chic and elegant from now on?

If yes, then look no further: This book is tailored for you!

The fashion industry and most style authors assume that all plus sized women are the same shape. Wrong!

Marie-Anne Lecoeur acknowledges that plus sized women also come in different shapes.

The advice in each chapter of this book is carefully tailored to the five main body shapes: APPLE, PEAR, HOURGLASS, INVERTED TRIANGLE and RECTANGLE.

From the foundations of shapewear to clothes and accessories, Marie-Anne Lecoeur gives detailed and specific assistance to help you transform your sense of style forever.

Why wait any longer? Make the most of your figure and look sensational today!

Pear Shape: Daywear Mini-Guide

Not sure how to make the most of your shape?
Don't know your do's from your don'ts?
At a loss about choosing what to wear?

If you do not know which clothes will make you
look fabulous and which won't, this pear shape
mini-guide will show you.

Marie-Anne Lecoeur shows you how you can attain the chic and elegance that French women seem to exude.

Pear Shape is direct and to the point, with no waffle or extra padding.

You will no longer waste your hard-earned cash on clothes that do not work for you. You will discover how to choose the right clothes for your shape.

Here are just a few of the many questions answered:

Which popular item should not be worn by pears?

Which past decade is pear-licious, and why?

Why avoiding this feature will make you lose inches on your hips and bottom?

Do not let your shape stop you from becoming the new chic and elegant you!

The Tidy Closet

Are you stuck in a rut and in despair over your untidy closet?
Do you want your clothes to show you off to your best advantage?
Do you lack motivation and know-how?
Are you crying out for a helping hand?

Marie-Anne Lecoeur draws from her life in France to give you simple advice and tips to motivate you to declutter and tidy your closet today.

You will get the following:

Motivation to get you started
Step by step advice on decluttering
Organisation ideas
Bonus chapter on how to create a classic wardrobe with essentials that work
Exercises
Tips
And much, much more

On reading this book, you will discover the hows and whys of the clutterer's mind. You will feel motivated to tidy and declutter your closet. You will learn how to create and organise a Chic wardrobe, just like a French woman.

Follow Marie-Anne's simple instructions and start tidying your closet today!

Acknowledgements

I would like to thank my husband Carl for his unending support, my sister Christiane for helping edit my drafts, my family and friends for being as excited as me about this project, and of course my mother who taught me all about chic and elegance.

A special thank you to Lakeland.co.uk and Joanne from Tallgirls.co.uk

Before You Go

I hope that this book has inspired and motivated you to be chic and elegant. If you have enjoyed the tips given, kindly consider writing a review online. Positive reviews give authors the encouragement they need to continue writing. Merci beaucoup.

A Bientôt

Marie-Anne Lecoeur

www.howtobechicandelegant.com

Illustration Credits

Cover
© Can Stock Photo Inc. / Oksvik

Introduction
© Can Stock Photo Inc. / pinkpig

General Tips
© Can Stock Photo Inc. / pinkpig

Body Shapes
© Can Stock Photo Inc. / V_rGi

Clothes
© Can Stock Photo Inc. / chinchilla

Lingerie
© Can Stock Photo Inc. / Blondinka89

Shoes
© Can Stock Photo Inc. / ivaleksa

Accessories
© Can Stock Photo Inc. / lenm

Skin
© Can Stock Photo Inc. / gurus

Make-up
© Can Stock Photo Inc. / GearKTV

Hands and Nails
© Can Stock Photo Inc. / JackyBrown

Hair
© Can Stock Photo Inc. / mallinka

Conclusion
© Can Stock Photo Inc. / GeraKTV